THE SECRET PLACE OF
THUNDER

UNDERSTANDING AND HARNESSING
THE POWER OF PRAYER

RICHARD THOMPSON

21st Century Christian

ISBN: 978-0-89098-496-3

©2013 by 21st Century Christian
2809 12th Ave S, Nashville, TN 37204
All rights reserved.

Unless otherwise noted Scripture quotations are from the English Standard Version.
Scripture quotations are from The Holy Bible, English Standard Version® (ESV®),
copyright © 2001 by Crossway, a publishing ministry of Good News Publishers.
Used by permission. All rights reserved.

Cover design by Jonathan Edelhuber

Table Of Contents

Foreword

Have you ever struggled with prayer? I mean *really* struggled with prayer? Maybe you went a week and just forgot to pray. Or despite your best intentions, perhaps you dozed off in the middle of your prayer without finishing. Have you ever felt no one was listening, like you were only talking to a wall? Or maybe you felt you were just saying the same old rambling things, day after day and night after night.

Each of these things could have applied to my prayer life just a few years ago. I knew prayer was important, and I tried to be consistent and at least go through the motions. But at its best, my prayer life was sporadic, unfocused, mostly selfish, and pretty boring. To use a good old Southern expression, my prayer life "stunk out loud." In fact, I finally became so exasperated with the poor quality of my prayer life that I called "time out." I prayed simply to improve the quality of my prayer life. I determined to spend one full year reading through the Bible and studying every passage that mentioned prayer, to better understand and appreciate what prayer is all about. This book is a result of that undertaking.

Now, several years later, my life has been transformed by prayer. I currently spend a great deal of time in daily prayer and feel "cheated" if, for some reason, I don't get to indulge in my relationship with God. I strive to have a regular time and place for substantial prayer, but also pray multiple times throughout the day as the need arises. I maintain an extensive prayer list that I take before the Father regularly, and can't read the newspaper without adding to that list. I say this not to boast or brag about my prayer life, because it continues to need improvement, but to illustrate the dramatic impact this study of God's Word had on my life. I now see myself as a participant in God's work, impacting the lives of people I love, as well as ones I don't even know personally. And I have seen the results of my prayers firsthand, often with dramatic results.

If you are a prayer warrior, this book is not for you. Read something on another topic. But if you have struggled with prayer, as I have, I hope that sharing my learning with you will enable you to break out of that mundane prayer existence and allow you to begin to experience the dynamic prayer life that I now enjoy.

The psalmist Asaph described prayer in this way:

"In distress you called, and I delivered you;
I answered you in the secret place of thunder"
Psalm 81:7 (English Standard Version)

There is a place we can go known only to God and ourselves. We can take anything to this secret place, no matter how large or small it may be. There is power in this secret place, the power found in a thunderstorm. It is the place where God moves and acts to transform our lives and the lives of those around us.

Think about it. You have the capability to interact with the One who created all we see and know and to actually change events in human history! It's happened before and God has revealed it to us in His Word. So get a good cup of coffee or tea, grab your Bible, and read on to learn what prayer is all about, and how you can experience a dynamic, exciting, and fulfilling prayer life as you confidently approach the throne of God, and receive mercy and grace to help you in your time of need (Hebrews 4:16).

1

The Meaning of Prayer

So just what is prayer? When I was a small child, my father taught me a very appealing rhyme:

"Star light, star bright,
   First star I see tonight,
   I wish I may, I wish I might
   Have the wish I wish tonight."

The premise of this poem was that if you recite the rhyme when you first see a star in the evening, you can wish for anything you want and your wish will come true. That is, of course, if you don't tell anyone about your wish (which rarely happens!).

In my youthful innocence, I put quite a bit of faith in this approach. Unfortunately, many people approach prayer in that same way. But praying to God is vastly different from wishing on a star. Before we explore God's truth to learn about prayer, we first must understand the meaning of prayer itself.

The original meaning and use of the word *prayer* in the ancient biblical languages is in itself quite revealing. In the Old Testament, the Hebrews used the word *tephillah* for prayer, which basically means "to judge oneself." The Jews revered prayer as a time for introspection and examination of one's relationship with God. In the Bible, Abraham is the first person we have record of praying (Genesis 20:7). Here the word for pray is *palal*, which means "to ask mentally or officially." The word *sha'al* is also sometimes used, which means "to demand, beg, consult, or desire earnestly." Also the word *siyach*, which means "converse or utter," is sometimes used to refer to prayer that is verbal and audible.

In the New Testament there are three different Greek words which are translated as the word "prayer" in English. The first of these is *proseuchomai*, which means "to supplicate, worship, or make prayer." It is a compound word made up of pro, which specifies "direction or nearness to God" and *euchomai*, which means "to wish, will or desire." Thus, in prayer we get near to God to make our wishes or desires known to Him.

A second Greek word that is translated prayer is *parakaleo*. This is also a compound word. *Para* means "near, beside, or equal" and *kaleo* means "to call or bid." Together these words mean "to call someone who is on an equal level with us." Jesus used this word when He asked Satan, "Do you think that I cannot now appeal to my Father, and He will at once send Me more than twelve legions of angels?" (Matthew 26:53). Jesus was able to use this word because He is on a par or equal with God and man, which qualifies Him to be a mediator between ourselves and God.

The third Greek word for prayer is *deomai*, which means "to beg or petition as binding oneself." This word designates an urgent need and connotes the idea of begging or petitioning God, while offering or binding ourselves as a means of answer to prayer. Jesus used this word when He told the disciples to "pray earnestly to the Lord of the harvest to send out laborers into His harvest" (Matthew 9:38).

Thus, prayer should be a very dynamic and interactive activity on the part of both us and God. It is not a mindless repetition of flowery language, nor is it a "wish I may" or "wish I might" pot shot at getting something we want or need to happen. Jesus said, "And whatever you ask in prayer, you will receive, if you have faith" (Matthew 21:22). The Hebrew writer describes how Christians, cleansed by the blood of Christ, can approach the throne of God with boldness and confidence (Hebrews 4:16). These statements are not a money-back guarantee that everything we request in prayer we will receive, but they demonstrate the power we have to approach God and participate in the development of future events, both in our own lives and in the lives of others. The remainder of this study will examine what the Bible teaches us about prayer and the remarkable things that have happened in human history as a result of ordinary people's interaction with their Creator in faith. With God, all things are possible!

References 1-7

http://www.searchgodsword.org/lex/heb/view.cgi?number=08605

http://www.searchgodsword.org/lex/heb/view.cgi?number=06419

http://www.searchgodsword.org/lex/heb/view.cgi?number=07592

http://www.searchgodsword.org/lex/heb/view.cgi?number=07878

http://www.searchgodsword.org/lex/grk/view.cgi?number=04336

http://www.searchgodsword.org/lex/grk/view.cgi?number=03870

http://www.searchgodsword.org/lex/grk/view.cgi?number=01189

3/5/17
- being mindful
  - taking a "time out" to take inventory
    of our lives
- how to do things better

Heb. 4:16
  - approach God's throne of
    grace w/ confidence (boldly)

Mt. 6:5-15
Rev. 22:20

- describe prayer to others?
  - earnest asking
  - transparency; vulnerability

2

The Nature of Prayer

What does the Bible tell us about the nature of prayer itself? Numerous passages describe very basic characteristics of prayer. The Bible also tells us what prayer does for us from a functional point of view and how God receives and responds to prayer. Several passages also warn us of the negative impact sin in our life can have on the effectiveness of our prayer. Let's examine each of these aspects more closely.

Characteristics of Prayer

Several passages in the Bible describe prayer in a variety of ways, but perhaps the most fundamental, necessary characteristic of prayer is purity. As Job is grappling with the grief of his loss and the misguided counsel and insensitivity of his three friends, he states:

"My face is red with weeping,
   and on my eyelids is deep darkness,
   although there is no violence in my hands,
   and my prayer is pure" (Job 16:16-17).

When we go before our Creator in prayer, there can be no pretentiousness. All is laid bare before Him. Our thoughts, our desires, our motives are all exposed in His presence. We must be willing and able to acknowledge who He is and who we are, when we approach His glorious throne. That perspective will direct our prayer in such a way as to maximize its effectiveness. If we are truly seeking His will in our lives, rather than our own, our prayers are much more likely to be answered.

As we see with Job, prayer is often characterized by emotion. While in the depths of despair in Babylonian exile, Jeremiah describes the response of the Israelites to God's declaration of restoration and salvation as singing, shouting, praise, weeping, and prayer (Jeremiah 31:7-9). Their communication in response to God's message was a literal emotional roller coaster.

Is our prayer life often characterized by such emotion? Or do we feel compelled to adhere to the constraints we impose on public prayer, even in our personal quiet time with God? I believe you've never really prayed until you've done so while crying your eyes out. God gave us emotions, and when our raw honesty pours through them, it creates an intimacy with Him like nothing else.

We see this intimacy as Jesus prays to His Father in Gethsemane (Mark 14:32-42). He fell on the ground to pray. He is described as "deeply distressed and troubled, overwhelmed with sorrow to the point of death." He clearly did not want to endure what lay ahead. Three times He asked His Father to remove this cup from Him. Luke adds that he was in anguish and His sweat was like great drops of blood falling down to the ground (Luke 22:44). Yet, ultimately, He desired God's will more than His own. Hallelujah! What a Savior!

In addition to being pure and emotional, our prayer should also be courageous and full of thanksgiving. The prophet Daniel is a great example of this (Daniel 6:10). When faced with a legal injunction punishable by death not to petition any god or man other than Darius for 30 days, Daniel not only continued his practice of praying three times daily, but did so with prayers of thanksgiving. Daniel clearly held his ongoing relationship with God as a higher priority than his own life. Did Daniel know that God would rescue him from the hungry lions? I doubt it. But he must have maintained the same attitude that the apostle Paul did when he wrote to the Philippians that for him, "to live is Christ, and to die is gain" (Philippians 1:21).

We are unlikely to be challenged today as Daniel was with the threat of death for praying. But how would we respond if we were? Is our prayer life such a priority that even a death threat would not hinder us? When we allow many minor things to disrupt and disengage our prayer relationship with the Father, it is an indicator that we do not fully understand the importance and the power of the access to God we have in the avenue of prayer. And if we do understand, like Daniel, we will be in praise and thanksgiving, no matter what circumstances we face.

Some characteristics of prayer relate to how and when we pray. God tells Jeremiah, "You will seek Me, and find Me when you seek Me with all your heart" (Jeremiah 29:13). Prayer takes effort! It is not something that we just casually slide in and out of. Peter encourages us to be "self-controlled and sober-minded" so that we may pray (1 Peter 4:7). And as we saw with Daniel, prayer should not be affected by our circumstances. James tells us we should pray in sickness and in trouble (James 5:13-15). Isaiah suggests we should pray even when God is disciplining us and we can only whisper to Him (Isaiah 26:16).

While we often think of prayer as a personal, individual act before God, the Bible also emphasizes the shared nature of prayer. James teaches that Christians have an obligation to pray for one another (James 5:16). It is also appropriate for a Christian to pray for the sin of another unrighteous person when they are penitent. For example, Job was asked by God to pray for his accusers that their sin might be forgiven (Job 42:7-9).

While we can meet this obligation in personal private prayer, there is tremendous power in praying together with other Christians. This can take the form of a dedicated relationship with another brother or sister for prayer or with an entire group of Christians who meet to pray together. Paul pleaded with the Roman Christians to "strive together with me in your prayers to God on my behalf" (Romans 15:30-33).

Finally, a couple of negative characteristics of prayer should be noted. It is possible to direct prayer other than to God. Isaiah describes an idol maker who prays to his handmade idol (Isaiah 44:17). This is futile, of course, since only God has the power to answer prayer. But we should be careful not to depend upon direction or answers or solutions from sources other than God. There are many available sources of guidance in the world today that might offer to provide such direction for us.

Another intriguing aspect of prayer is that failure to pray is sin. Samuel told the people of Israel, "Far be it from me that I should sin against the Lord by ceasing to pray for you" (1 Samuel 12:23). Perhaps this derives from the original meaning of sin as "missing the mark." God desires for us to be in prayer for one another. Failing to do so "misses the mark." James puts it this way, "So whoever knows the right thing to do and fails to do it, for him it is sin" (James 4:17). The implications of this are quite profound. Whenever we are made aware of needs that can be addressed with prayer, we have an obligation as Christians to do so.

How Prayer Works

In addition to these descriptions of the characteristics of prayer, the Bible also explains how prayer works. Several Scriptures describe what prayer does for us or how it functions on our behalf. Numerous other

Scriptures describe God's response to prayer in a number of ways.

One of the most important functions of prayer is to bring us into the presence of our Creator and draw God near to us. Moses described the nation of Israel as set apart from all others because the Lord God was near to them "whenever we call upon Him" (Deuteronomy 4:7). As Elihu instructed Job in his rebuke, "Then man prays to God and He accepts him; he sees His face with a shout of joy, and He restores to man His righteousness" (Job 33:26). Prayer provides not only access to God, but acceptance by Him as well.

In God's presence and with His acceptance, it is possible for God's will to be revealed. This is certainly how Peter was informed of God's acceptance of the Gentiles as His children (Acts 10:9-17). While this may appear to be a "special" intervention because Peter fell into a trance while praying, it may also speak to the depth of our prayer interaction with God and our willingness to hear His will for our lives.

Most of us probably view the utility of prayer as a means to an end. We need something done, so we ask God for it. This is particularly true in cases of human infirmity and suffering. And this is not inappropriate. James encouraged the early Christians, "Is anyone among you suffering? Let them pray. Is anyone cheerful? Let him sing praise. Is anyone among you sick? Let him call for the elders of the church, and let them pray over him anointing him with oil in the name of the Lord. And the prayer of faith will save the one who is sick, and the Lord will raise him up. And if he has committed sins, he will be forgiven" (James 5:13-15).

But this healing power of prayer extends beyond the physical realm. Mark describes the healing of a mute boy with an unclean spirit (Mark 9:25-27). When the disciples asked why they were unable to drive the spirit out, Jesus replied, "This kind cannot be driven out by anything but prayer" (vs. 29).

While we tend to focus a great deal on the physical benefits of prayer, it has powerful spiritual effects as well. In Gethsemane, Jesus encouraged His disciples, "Watch and pray that you may not enter into temptation. The spirit indeed is willing, but the flesh is weak" (Mark 14:38). As Jesus demonstrated a model prayer, He said, "And lead us not into temptation, but deliver us from evil" (Matthew 6:13). Do we pray as much for the spiritual well-being of ourselves and others as for our physical well-being?

Prayer even has the ability to make things holy or "set apart." Timothy spoke of this in the context of food, from which certain false teachers were requiring abstinence (1 Timothy 4:3-5). He pointed out that everything created by God is good and nothing is to be rejected if it is received with thanksgiving. "For everything created by God is good, and nothing is to be rejected if it is received with thanksgiving, for it is made holy by the word of God and prayer."

God's Response To Prayer

Does it ever seem like you are praying to a blank wall? Does a lack of immediate response create a sense of futility in your prayer life? As a rule, we Americans are not a patient people. We live in a fast-food world and generally want everything yesterday. But God doesn't always operate with the same urgency we might desire. Think about it. Does the Creator of the universe really need you to tell Him about what needs here on earth He should address? Isn't He omniscient and already aware of the situation? Or does He simply allow us to participate in the process perhaps as much for our needs as for the needs of those for whom we pray?

It took me a long time to understand the parable of the persistent widow (Luke 18:1-8). Why would God want us to continually pray about the same thing over and over again? Doesn't He already know anyway? What is the point in being repetitious in our prayer?

The point is that we continue to rely upon Him and maintain our faith regardless of the status of our response from God. Since I have developed a much deeper understanding of prayer, I have now prayed for some things regularly for periods of over one year before seeing those prayers answered. The intensity of the effort helps me to better appreciate the response I get from God. And often the circumstances change or are modified significantly over time such that the prayer request itself actually changes in accordance with the answer that God ultimately provides. This may be analogous to taking a long trip, where often the majority of the benefit is in the process of getting there, rather than arriving at the final destination.

But in those times when prayer might seem futile, the Bible reassures us that God does in fact hear our prayers. "The Lord is far from the wicked, but He hears the prayer of the righteous" (Proverbs 15:29). "He regards the prayer of the destitute and does not despise their prayer" (Psalm 102:17). In fact, God apparently is pleased by and respective of the appearance of our prayers before Him. The prayers of Cornelius ascended as a memorial offering before God (Acts 10:4). And numerous passages indicate that God receives prayer as if it were incense (Psalm 141:2; Revelation 5:8; Revelation 8:3-4).

When we go before God in prayer, we can expect to receive an answer. As Paul instructed Philemon, we should go ahead and take action expectant of the answer to our prayer (Philemon 22). James noted that the prayer of a righteous person is both powerful and effective (James 5:16-18). This is no small claim. In fact, even when we are inadequate to express a need in prayer, God provides His Holy Spirit to intercede for us (Romans 8:26-27). Realizing and claiming the power at our disposal in prayer should allow us to approach life from an entirely different perspective and truly participate in the divine nature as we live in a fallen and lost world.

But there are a couple of caveats. God's answer to our prayer depends upon the attitude of our hearts (Psalm 66:16-20). When we cry out to Him and praise Him, He listens. If we cherish sin in our hearts, He doesn't. It also depends upon our faith. "And whatever you ask in prayer, you will receive if you have faith" (Matthew 21:22).

There are also important caveats regarding the ultimate effect our prayer can have. There are examples of negative effects from prayer when not offered from the proper perspective. Prayer can condemn us (Psalm 109:7). Prayer from an improper perspective can also engender God's anger (Psalm 80:4). Sin itself may well be the reason a prayer is not being answered.

The Effect of Sin On Prayer

The Bible provides several examples of unanswered prayer due to sin. King David experienced this in his encounter with the Gibeonites in 2 Samuel 21:1-14. There was a three-year famine underway in Israel and David sought the face of the Lord. God made it clear to David that the famine was a result of "Saul and his blood-stained house...because he put the Gibeonites to death." The people of Israel had sworn to spare them, but Saul, in his zeal, had killed them. This sin was responsible for the famine, despite the pleas of the people for the land. David turned over seven of Saul's sons to the remaining Gibeonites to be hanged for atonement. Once this was accomplished and their bodies were buried with the bones of Saul and Jonathan, God responded to the plea for the land.

Another example is given in Lamentations 3. In Babylonian exile Jeremiah bemoans the spiritual condition of Judah. In verse 8 he laments, "though I call and cry for help, He shuts out my prayer." The reason is made clear in verses 42-44: "We have transgressed and rebelled and you have not forgiven. You have wrapped yourself with anger and pursued us; Killing without pity. You have wrapped yourself with a cloud so that no prayer can pass through."

These clear examples should give us pause whenever we experience a lack of response from God in prayer. He may simply desire us to be patient and persistent. But we should ensure that the problem doesn't lie with us, because of unrepentant sin. Sin can be quite insidious and doesn't have to be on the magnitude of murder or idolatry to impede prayer. Peter points out that something as simple as the way husbands treat their wives can be sufficient to hinder their prayers (1 Peter 3:7).

The effect of sin on prayer appears to be quite profound. Solomon declares, "If one turns away his ear from hearing the law, even his prayer is an abomination" (Proverbs 28:9). God told Judah through the prophet Isaiah, "When you spread out your hands, I will hide my eyes from you; even though you make many prayers, I will not listen; your hands are full of blood" (Isaiah 1:15). Frequency of prayer doesn't matter when sin is present. Neither does fervency. Isaiah also says, "And when Moab presents himself, When he wearies himself on the high place; when he goes to his sanctuary to pray, he will not prevail" (Isaiah 16:12). Jeremiah was even instructed by God not to intercede or pray for sinful Judah (Jeremiah 7:16; 11:14).

It should be clear that these passages are referring to unrepentant sin. God surely will hear the prayer of a repentant sinner. It's when we refuse to acknowledge our sin or choose to persist in it, that it becomes a problem for our prayer life. In fact, it can lead us not to pray at all. As Job questioned the prosperity of the wicked, he pointed out, "They say to God, 'Depart from us! We do not desire the knowledge of Your ways. What is the Almighty, that we should serve Him? And what profit do we get if we pray to Him?' Behold, is not their prosperity in their hand, the counsel of the wicked is far from me" (Job 21:14-16).

3

The Focus of Prayer

Just as the Bible teaches us about the nature of prayer, it also addresses many things that should be the focus of our prayer. While it's fairly safe to say that nothing is too large or too small to bring before our Father in prayer, the Bible does enumerate several specific things for which we should pray. Generally, these can be divided into things we pray about for other people, things we pray about for other believers, and things we pray about for ourselves.

Prayer For Other People

People in the world at large have both physical and spiritual needs for which we should pray. Many may have personal needs that may benefit from our prayer. Paul tells Timothy how widows who are left all alone, continue in supplications and prayers night and day (1 Timothy 5:5). He also instructs Timothy to pray for all people, especially those who hold positions of power such as kings (1 Timothy 2:1-2). James reveals that Elijah prayed for the weather, first for drought, and later for rain (James 5:17-18). Ever wonder what to pray about for other people? Pick up a newspaper. You'll discover lots of needs that people have all around you that you can help them with through prayer.

In addition to these physical needs, people in the world at large are also in need of prayer for their spiritual needs. Of course, the greatest spiritual need is for people to be in a saving relationship with our Lord and Savior, Jesus Christ. Paul desired this for both Jews and Gentiles (Acts 26:29; Romans 10:1). Our concern for others' spiritual well-being should not be hindered by their attitude toward us. Both Jesus and Paul taught in numerous instances that we should pray for those who persecute us (Matthew 5:43-45; Luke 6:27-28; Acts 7:60). This would include praying for the forgiveness of others, as Stephen did while being stoned (Acts 7:59-60).

Prayer For Other Christians

We have a special responsibility to pray for our other brothers and sisters in Christ, and numerous specific instructions and examples are provided in God's Word. Again these include both physical and spiritual needs. Paul credited the prayer of many believers for the physical blessings that he received (2 Corinthians 1:11). Jesus' brother, James, instructed dispersed Jewish Christians to call the elders of the church for prayer when they are sick. He also instructs them to pray for each other for healing (James 5:14-16).

While it may be somewhat obvious that we should pray for other brothers or sisters in Christ with physical needs, there are actually many more passages in the Bible that encourage us to pray for their spiritual needs. In John 17, Jesus prayed not only for His disciples, but for "those who will believe in Me through their message." He prayed for their unity and for their protection from the evil one. Likewise, Paul prayed for and solicited prayers from the many churches that he encouraged (Colossians 1:3-5; 1 Thessalonians 1:2; 1 Thessalonians 5:25; Philemon 4-5). He prayed without ceasing for his Roman brothers and sisters (Romans 1:8-10).

We should pray for our other brothers' and sisters' knowledge and depth of understanding of their relationship with God through Jesus.

Paul encouraged Christians in both Ephesus and Colosse to pray for spiritual wisdom and understanding of God in others (Ephesians 1:15-23; Colossians 1:9). He also prayed for the Philippians' love to abound with knowledge and discernment (Philippians 1:9-10). Since God's Spirit is involved in this process, we should also pray for His activity in the lives of other Christians, as the apostles did in Acts 8:14.

We should pray for our other brothers and sisters not to do wrong, and for restoration when they do sin (2 Corinthians 13:7,9). Our struggle in this world is a spiritual one between the Spirit and our flesh, between forces of God and forces of evil. Jesus prayed in John 17 for protection of the believers from the evil one. He did not pray for their removal from this world of spiritual warfare, but rather for their victory over it though His death and the indwelling of the Holy Spirit.

This is the ultimate test of our faith. Paul prayed for the Thessalonians to supply what was lacking in their faith (1 Thessalonians 3:10) Jesus prayed for Peter's faith not to fail (Luke 22:31-32). (Satan had demanded to sift Peter like wheat). While Peter did fail soon after that by denying Jesus, his repentant life afterward included preaching the first gospel sermon, writing two epistles in the Bible, and suffering death as a martyr for Christ (John 21:19). When you look at the entirety of Peter's life, Jesus' prayer was answered.

Often when we do lose faith and sin, it may have long-lasting consequences for our lives. But fortunately we can ask other brothers and sisters to pray for us to avoid some of those consequences. Simon recognized this after attempting to buy the power of the Holy Spirit from Peter and requested prayer on his behalf (Acts 8:24). John, likewise, instructed Christians to pray for other brothers who commit sins not leading to death, that God will give them life (1 John 5:16).

Another area in which we should pray for other brothers and sisters in Christ is the effectiveness of their evangelism. In John 17, Jesus prayed to God for the unity of all believers so that "the world may believe that You have sent me." Jesus knew that Christian unity was essential for effective evangelism. Local leadership in the church is essential as well. As Paul appointed elders in every church, he prayed and fasted for their commitment to the Lord in whom they had believed (Acts 14:23).

Paul also prayed for the personal evangelistic efforts of his other brothers and sisters in Christ. He prayed for the Colossians to "Walk in a manner worthy of the Lord, fully pleasing to him, bearing fruit in every good work, and increasing in the knowledge of God" (Colossians 1:10). He asked both the Ephesian and Colossian churches to pray for him that the word might be proclaimed with boldness (Ephesians 6:18-20; Colossians 4:2-4). He prayed for the Philippians for their partnership in the gospel (Philippians 1:5). Since we share Jesus' mission to seek and save the lost, prayer for each other in that effort should be a priority in our daily prayer life.

Prayer For Ourselves

We also have a responsibility to pray for the needs we have ourselves. If you're like me, you probably do spend time praying for your own physical needs. But how often do we pray for our spiritual needs? Again, essentially all of what the Scriptures teach on this subject is directed toward spiritual, rather than physical, needs.

Paul asks the Roman Christians to "join me in my struggle by praying to God for me." He asks for prayer for rescue from unbelievers and acceptable service before God (Romans 15:30-33). He made similar requests and acknowledgements from the Corinthians, Philippians, and Thessalonians, as did the writer of Hebrews to his audience (2 Corinthains 1:11; Philippians 1:19; 2 Thessalonians 3:1; Hebrews 13:18). We can do this under any circumstance, no matter how extenuating. When Jesus foretold the fall of Jerusalem in Matthew 24, He instructed pregnant and nursing women to pray that their flight would not be during winter or on a Sabbath. David prayed continually against the evil deeds of his adversaries (Psalm 141:5). If we find ourselves in sin, we can repent and pray for forgiveness of the intent of our heart as Peter instructed Simon (Acts 8:22).

We can pray not to enter into temptation (Luke 22:40, 46). And during times of temptation, we can pray for strength with power through His Spirit in our inner being (Ephesians 3:14-21, Colossians 1:11). He does this according to the riches of His glory. That's a lot of power and strength! He does this so that Christ can dwell in our hearts through faith and so that we can comprehend the magnitude of Christ's love and be filled with all the fullness of God.

I have to confess that comprehending the full magnitude of the love of God, Jesus, and the Spirit is challenging. I'm not sure I will ever fully comprehend it in this life. However, it is encouraging to know that we can grow in our comprehension of it, as we are filled with God and He lives in us. And it is exciting to realize that it is His power that is at work within us. As Paul told the Colossian Christians, "For this I toil, struggling with all his energy that He powerfully works within me" (Colossians 1:29).

We should pray to be worthy of God's calling and to fulfill the purpose He has given us by allowing His power to work through us (2 Thessalonians 1:11). Of course, we will never actually be worthy. But that should be our desire, as we seek to serve Him to the best of our ability. We should seek to use the gifts He has blessed us with to serve Him. When Paul addressed Christians who spoke in tongues in the Corinthian church, he urged them to pray for the power to interpret what they were saying (1 Corinthians 14:13). I believe this is appropriate for any spiritual gift or talent we may be given. We should always pray to use it to the best of our ability and for the most benefit to the Lord. We should also pray for the effective sharing of our faith (Philemon 6). And we should pray to share it boldly (Acts 4:29).

Finally, we should pray for mercy. Our attitude before God should be like that of the tax collector: "God, be merciful to me, a sinner" (Luke 18:13). It is this attitude that is justified by God, not an attitude of pride or arrogance. The one who humbles himself will be exalted. We should pray to escape the things that will happen on this earth at the end of time (Luke 21:36). And, like Stephen, we should pray for Jesus to receive our spirit (Acts 7:59).

King David's prayer for his relationship with God was summarized in a very focused way in Psalm 27:4 "One thing I have asked of the LORD, that I will seek after: that I may dwell in the house of the LORD all the days of my life, to gaze upon the beauty of the LORD and to inquire in His temple." He also asked God to teach him and to lead him in a straight path. What a great example for us to follow as we pray for ourselves and our unique, individual relationship with God.

4

Prerequisites For Prayer

If you've ever taken any advanced-level college coursework, you're probably very familiar with the concept of prerequisites. Most advanced courses require that certain more elementary courses have been mastered, prior to enrolling in the advanced class. This is to ensure optimal learning and to prevent students from encountering undue difficulty in trying to master advanced material that they are not yet prepared to understand.

The Bible also speaks of certain qualities and characteristics that must be in place for prayer to be effective. Most of these qualities and characteristics relate to the attitude of our heart. Fortunately, there are not many prerequisites for prayer. However, the few that are addressed are important and worthy of our consideration in attempting to better understand what prayer is all about.

Humility

Whenever we approach God in prayer, we must do so with an attitude of humility. We must remember who we are and who God is. And we must be both grateful and thankful that He even allows us to come before His presence through Jesus. Anything else is arrogance before Him.

The Bible teaches both explicitly and through example the necessity of humility before God in prayer. After Solomon had dedicated the temple to God, the LORD appeared to him in the night and said, "I have heard your prayer and have chosen this place for myself as a house of sacrifice. When I shut up the heavens so that there is no rain, or command the locust to devour the land, or send pestilence among my people, if my people, who are called by my name, humble themselves, and pray and seek my face and turn from their wicked ways, then I will hear from heaven and will forgive their sin and heal their land" (2 Chronicles 7:12-14). The answer to their prayer was predicated upon humility among other things.

We also see this clearly by example in the New Testament with the striking contrast of the Pharisee and the tax collector (Luke 18:9-14). While the Pharisee bragged publicly about all that he did on God's behalf, the tax collector simply prayed, "God, be merciful to me, a sinner!" As Jesus explained the justification of the tax collector, He declared, "For everyone who exalts himself will be humbled, but the one who humbles himself will be exalted." He also warned His disciples of scribes who liked to walk around in long robes and be greeted in the marketplace and have the best seats in the synagogue and places of honor at feasts (Luke 20:46). They were cited for condemnation as well. Thus an attitude of humility is a must when seeking God in prayer.

Repentance

In addition to humility, a repentant heart is required to go before God in prayer. We established in Chapter One that one characteristic of prayer is that it can be hindered by sin. Since we all sin and fall short of the glory of God, it follows that a repentant heart is also a necessary prerequisite for prayer. A repentant heart grows out of the attitude of humility that is also required.

In the previous example of God appearing to Solomon at the

dedication of the temple, three contingencies were placed upon God's response to their prayers. One was an attitude of humility, as previously discussed. Another was to pray and seek His face. The third contingency was to "turn from their wicked ways" (2 Chronicles 7:12-14). God made it very clear that if these conditions were not met, their prayers would not be heard in heaven. Thus repentance is also a necessary prerequisite before approaching God in prayer.

Obedience

In this same passage, God declares that His favor upon the people is dependent upon their obedience. Certainly that would impact His responsiveness to prayer as well. Of course, none of us will ever be 100% obedient because of our depraved, sinful nature. We have all sinned and fall short of the glory of God (Romans 3:23). However, there is a difference in seeking to be obedient wholeheartedly, but occasionally failing, versus not really trying to be obedient in the first place. God knows the intent of our hearts and our lives reflect the sincerity of our commitment to obedience.

Forgiveness

Perhaps one of the most difficult prerequisites for prayer for humans is the requirement that we forgive others who have sinned against us. Given the right circumstances and significant consequences, most people are ultimately willing to humble themselves before God and repent. When it comes to forgiveness, however, many people cling to their past hurt and nurture it for years, rather than simply offering forgiveness to the hurtful person.

In Mark 11:25, Jesus makes it clear that forgiveness is a prerequisite for effective prayer. In fact, our forgiveness from God is contingent upon our willingness to forgive others. While this may sound easy from a simple reading of the text, anyone who has been deeply hurt by another human being can testify that this may be one of the more difficult things we are asked to accomplish as humans. But it is necessary for our prayer to be effective. In another context, Jesus suggests that we leave our gifts at the altar and go be reconciled to whomever has offended us before we make our gift to God (Matthew 5:23-24). Many people want to wait for the other person to come to them, but that is not what Jesus is suggesting here. We have an obligation to forgive and seek forgiveness, and failure to do so can be a huge impediment in our relationship with God, especially as we seek His presence in prayer.

Courage

In addition to humility, repentance, obedience, and forgiveness, truly effective prayer requires courage. This may seem surprising since access to God is so readily available and we can pray to God about anything at any time. However, the effort and intensity of our prayer that is needed may require a great deal of courage. This could be difficult in times of distress or defeat. But recognizing the power of God and the hope we have in Him can lift us out of whatever turmoil we may be facing, to give us the necessary courage to pray.

David recognized this in 1 Chronicles 17:25. David had intent to build a house for God (a temple). But God told him through Nathan the prophet, that it was the other way around. God would build a house for David. (Of course, he was referring to the work of His Son, Jesus, in establishing an eternal home for all who believe in Him). This realization had a major impact upon the quality of David's prayer life. As he expressed it, "You, my God, have revealed to your servant that you will build a house for him. Therefore your servant has found courage to pray before you."

We need to cultivate the same response to our understanding of

God in our daily prayer lives. If we truly recognize and appreciate the wonderful blessings we have in Christ, how can our prayers be anything but courageous before God? This is the attitude the writer of Hebrews reflected when he instructed us to approach the throne of God with "boldness and confidence." We do this, not because of ourselves and our ability to pray, but because of God and His ability to deliver and answer our prayers. God forgive us for failing to recognize this and offering up timid and weak whimpers of prayers laced with unbelief.

5

How To Pray

One of the most practical aspects of prayer is simply how it should be accomplished. Should prayer be private, public, or both? When should we pray? Where should we pray? In what position should we pray? How long should we pray? Believe it or not, the Bible actually addresses all of these issues. I don't mean to infer that there is only one acceptable way to pray, based on biblical standards. I really believe God will accept prayer of any nature, time, place, position, or length as long as it is sincere. However, the fact that these issues are actually addressed in the text suggests to me that some of these forms of prayer may be optimal and perhaps more effective for us than others.

A Place to Pray

Much attention is given in the Bible to the location of prayer, both public and private. Prayer can take place anywhere, as evidenced by Paul and Silas, who prayed while they were in jail (Acts 16:25). We also find women in Acts 16:13-16 who regularly went down by the riverside to pray. Early Christians commonly met together in homes to pray (Acts 4:24; 12:1-17).

But certain places can be special places for prayer. As Jesus threw the money-changers out of the temple, he quoted Isaiah saying, "My house shall be called a house of prayer, but you make it a den of robbers" (Matthew 21:13; Mark 11:17; Luke 19:46; Isaiah 56:7). Jews commonly went to the temple for the purpose of prayer (Luke 1:10; 18:9-14). And the apostles continued to pray at the temple even after Jesus had ascended to heaven (Acts 3:1; 22:17). Thus, public places of worship may offer unique environments that foster closeness to God and expedite our prayer.

While there is clearly a time and a place for public prayer, much more is said in Scripture about our private time in prayer. Prayer, ultimately, is the most private act we can engage in, as we converse with our Creator one-on-one. Jesus instructed His disciples to go into their room and shut the door to pray (Matthew 6:6). Often during His ministry, He would go off by himself to desolate places or mountains to pray (Matthew 14:23; Mark 1:35; 6:46; Luke 5:16; 6:12; 9:18,28; 11:1). Even facing death, He separated Himself first from the apostles at large, and then from His three closest followers in order to pray (Matthew 26:36; Mark 14:32-42; Luke 22:41). And the apostles continued this practice after Jesus had ascended back into heaven (Acts 9:40). Peter even went so far as to go up on the roof of a house to be alone to pray (Acts 10:9). Each of these situations teaches us that where we pray is very important. We must be in a place where we will and be able to focus and give our full attention to our prayer and not be interrupted.

When to Pray

There are several references in the Bible to when we should pray, both in respect to time and events. Jesus typically got up early in the morning to pray, as we see in Mark 1:35. Heman the Ezrahite did this as well (Psalm 88:13). Cornelius, on the other hand, was praying in his house at 3:00 p.m. (Acts 10:30). This was a typical time for Jewish prayer. David prayed evening, morning, and noon (Psalm 55:17). Likewise, the disciples of John fasted and prayed often (Luke 5:33). This is in agreement with the apostle Paul's later exhortation to "pray without ceasing." (1 Thessalonians 5:17). Certainly prayer is appropriate at any time of the day or night, but most of us are at our best at a particular time, usually morning or evening. That's the time when our prayer will be the deepest and likely most effective.

There are also certain events mentioned in the Bible associated with prayer. Jesus prayed at His baptism (Luke 3:21-22). James recommended prayer during times of suffering and sickness (James 5:13-15). While these more critical events may readily evoke prayer, it is very important to establish a habit of prayer and to designate a regular time and place for prayer. As mentioned previously, the Jews typically went to the temple at 3:00 p.m. to pray, and Jesus' disciples continued this practice (Acts 3:1). A primary characteristic of the early disciples was their devotion to prayer (Acts 1:14; 2:42; 6:4). Paul even advocated abstaining from sex for a period of devotion to prayer (1 Corinthians 7:5). Good prayer doesn't just develop by chance. Like most things in life, it must be planned for and cultivated in order to develop a deep and meaningful relationship with God. But the rewards of this effort are great. God is good and responds to those who earnestly seek Him.

How to Pray

The Bible also gives us much insight into how we should pray, both in regard to physical methods as well as to our mental and emotional attitudes. Several physical methods of prayer are described throughout the Bible. Jesus prayed for children by physically laying his hands upon them (Matthew 19:13). It appears the early apostles followed this practice as well (Acts 6:6). The practice of fasting along with prayer was used for events of significance, such as the setting apart of Barnabas and Saul for their missionary work (Acts 13:3). And in Old Testament times, Daniel wore sackcloth and ashes, physical evidence of grieving, in addition to fasting with his prayer (Daniel 9:3-23). Each of these examples illustrate how things we do physically can enhance our prayer life, whether it be touching someone, abstaining from something, or dressing in way that reminds us of our purpose.

Much is also said in the Bible regarding the position in which we pray. The most common position that is referenced in Scripture is falling to the ground in prayer, either kneeling or face down. This is a position of humility. The three gospels describe Jesus praying in this position at Gethsemane (Matthew 26:39; Mark 14:32-35; Luke 22:41). Stephen, Peter, and Paul prayed in this position as well (Acts 7:60; 9:40-41; 20:36; 21:5). But Moses has the record. Moses prayed face down on the ground for 40 days and nights for Aaron and the Israelites after they made the golden calf idol (Deuteronomy 9:25). Ezra stood up at the evening sacrifice, tore his clothes, fell to his knees and spread out his hands before God to pray (Ezra 9:5-15). But Hezekiah, (evidently too sick to get out of bed), simply turned his face to the wall to pray (2 Kings 20:2). The position of the body is probably not as important as the condition of the heart. Prostrate prayer simply evidences a contrite and humble heart before God.

But there are also examples of praying in an upright posture in the Bible. Jesus prayed lifting up His eyes to heaven (John 17:1). Paul instructed Timothy for men to pray "lifting holy hands without anger or quarreling" (1 Timothy 2:8). Paul also supported the maintenance of traditions in prayer, such as men praying with uncovered heads and women praying with covered heads (1 Corinthians 11:2-16).

Probably more important than these physical characteristics of prayer are our mental and emotional attitudes in prayer. As stated earlier, good prayer doesn't just happen by chance. Like most other things in life, it is achieved through effort and discipline. We should have specific purposes in mind when we pray, as opposed to just praying in generalities. Paul illustrated this in his prayers for the Thessalonian Christians (2 Thessalonians 1:11). One way of achieving this is to keep a list of prayer needs and removing them as prayers are answered. Paul encouraged the Phillipian Christians to "not be anxious about anything, but in everything by prayer and supplication with thanksgiving, let your requests be made known to God" (Philippians 4:6).

In addition to a sharp mental focus in our prayer, our emotional and spiritual involvement is important as well. James instructed dispersed Jewish Christians to pray fervently (James 5:17). Paul instructed the Roman and Corinthian Christians to "strive together with me in your prayers to God on my behalf" and "while they long for you and pray for you" (Romans 15:30; 2 Corinthians 9:12-15). All of these words imply a deep sense of emotional involvement in prayer. In fact, the intensity of our prayer should increase with the intensity of the need for which we are praying. Luke records that Jesus, being in agony, prayed more earnestly (Luke 22:44).

There are numerous examples of emotional expression in prayer. Perhaps the best example is that of Jesus in Gethsemane as recorded by three of the gospel writers (Matthew 26:38; Mark 14:33; Luke 22:44). The Hebrew writer alludes to this as well (Hebrews 5:7). Hezekiah prayed weeping bitterly to overcome his fatal condition (2 Kings 20:3). The Psalmists express prayer in this way as well (Psalm 61, 63, 84, 88, 102). As Stephen was dying, he called out to Jesus in a loud voice (Acts 7:60). Becoming emotional in prayer is nothing to be ashamed of or embarrassed about. Rather, it reflects the unpretentious prayer that God so desires (Mark 12:40; Luke 20:46).

These passages illustrate that effective prayer is a product of both the mind and the spirit. Paul made this very point when he wrote the Corinthians to address issues concerning speaking in tongues (1 Corinthians 14:13-17). Fortunately, those in Christ have His Holy Spirit living in them to assist with this. Jude instructed Christians to pray in the Holy Spirit (Jude 20). When we don't even know what to pray for, the Spirit intercedes for us with groanings too deep for words (Romans 8:26).

How Long to Pray

The Bible addresses the question of how long to pray from two different perspectives. One perspective is how long each individual prayer should be. The other perspective is how long we should continually pray about a certain issue. Let's explore what the Bible says about each of these perspectives.

There is no set criterion for the length of an individual prayer. Brief prayers are certainly acceptable and praying for unnecessarily long periods of time does not make a prayer more acceptable. Indeed, Jesus condemned those who made long prayers for a pretense (Luke 20:45-47). This probably had more to do with the attitude of their hearts than with the temporal aspect of their prayer. However, when faced with critical decisions, we do have an example of lengthy prayer being required. On the evening prior to selecting his twelve apostles, Jesus spent an entire evening in prayer (Luke 6:12).

A sustained, concerted effort in prayer is likely more important than the number of minutes or hours spent on any single prayer. Paul instructed Christians to be constant in prayer (Romans 12:12; Colossians 4:2; 1 Thessalonians 5:17). This was practiced under Judaism as well (Psalm 88:1). Paul certainly practiced praying without ceasing for other brothers and sisters in Christ (Romans 1:8-10; Philippians 1:3-4; Colossians 1:3,9; 1 Thessalonians 3:10; 2 Timothy 1:3). And there are other examples of persistent prayers as well: Anna, the prophetess (Luke 2:37) and Cornelius (Acts 10:2). Even Jesus prayed multiple times for His deliverance at Gethsemane (Matthew 26:36-45; Mark 14:32-42).

One of the most intriguing parables in the Bible is the parable of the persistent widow found in Luke 18:1-8. Jesus taught His disciples this parable for the express purpose of encouraging them to be constant in prayer and not lose heart. In this parable a widow comes to a judge requesting justice. The judge neither fears God nor respects man. The implication is that the judge really doesn't care about the widow's injustice, but because of her persistence, grants her request. Jesus declares that, similarly, God will give justice to His elect who cry to Him day and night. In fact, Jesus states that God's response will come more quickly because of the persistence of the petitioner. He ultimately links the widow's persistence to a demonstration of faith. Do we have the depth of faith to persist in prayer as this proverbial widow did?

A few years ago my sister asked me to pray for her to find a home to purchase. She had been living in a condominium for several years and was ready to purchase her first house. I prayed for this daily for approximately two years. After the first few months, I was somewhat disappointed that my prayer was not being readily answered. I couldn't figure this out. I knew her desire was appropriate and surely something God would bless. I also felt my prayers were sincere and offered in faith. But no answer was forthcoming.

What I did not know in those first few months was that in the following year, my family and I would be relocated to the same city my sister lived in, and she would ultimately buy a house very near to us. God knew and was planning all along for this to happen, but I had no clue at the time that any such thing could ever take place. I think this is why persistence in prayer is so important. The answer may be forthcoming, but not necessarily in the time frame that we expect.

The Reality of Prayer

There are few things about the reality of the nature of prayer itself that are pertinent to how we pray. For instance, Jesus taught in Matthew 6:8, that God knows our needs before we ask. Yet in Matthew 7:7, He tells us that we should ask, seek, and knock and those things we seek will be given to us. Why should we ask if He already knows what we need?

Prayer is not as much for God as it is for us. In a sense, it is a reflection of our faith. Jesus taught that to receive what we pray for, we must believe that we will receive it (Mark 11:24). Also, since we are not God and unable to fully ascertain what might be best, we should always ask for things in accordance with God's will (Matthew 26:39; Mark 14:36; Luke 22:42). What we desire may not be what God desires, as was the case with Christ in the garden of Gethsemane.

Also, good prayer is something that can be learned. Jesus provided a great example for us when He taught His disciples how to pray (Luke 11:1-13). Prayer should begin with praise for God and His kingdom. Prayer should embrace both our physical and our spiritual sustenance. (Just as we need food and drink on a daily basis, we also need and must give forgiveness). Prayer should also include an awareness of our spiritual battle and equip us for the fight. As noted previously, persistence in prayer will be rewarded. And perhaps most importantly, it is the Spirit that intercedes for us, and we should be asking for His presence in our lives.

6

Prayer For Physical And Emotional Strength

M any Scriptures in the Bible refer to prayer for physical and emotional strength. Sickness is a great common denominator among mankind. Who has not suffered some physical infirmity or emotional upset, even if just for a brief time? I find it comforting to know that God cares about our physical and emotional health and desires us to approach Him about it. He has the power to provide full and complete healing. He also has the patience to let us learn through suffering. Has anyone in history ever suffered more than God's own Son? He clearly desired relief from His suffering, yet prayed, "Not my will, but Yours be done" (Luke 22:42).

Prayer for Physical Strength

Samson prayed for physical strength to avenge himself against the Philistines for taking his eyesight (Judges 16:29). Does this seem like an unlikely prayer for God to answer—a prayer for revenge? A little context is helpful here. The setting for this great event was a sacrifice to the Philistine god, Dagon. The Philistines were celebrating Dagon's perceived delivery of Samson into their hands. They were also mocking Samson (and God) by asking Samson to provide entertainment for the evening. As a result of the answer to this prayer, Samson killed more Philistines in his death than he did in his life. God was serious when He said, "You shall have no other gods before me" (Exodus 20:3).

Nehemiah also prayed for his hands to be strengthened to rebuild the wall of Jerusalem (Nehemiah 6:9). This was in response to Sanballet's scare tactics to persuade Nehemiah to stop building. The wall had lain broken and burnt for many, many years. A loss of momentum would surely prevent the wall from being rebuilt. Yet, in response to Nehemiah's prayer, the rest of the Jews pitched in and the wall was completed in a mere fifty-two days.

Prayer for Emotional Strength

Sometimes our greatest challenges are not physical, but emotional. The Bible also provides us with examples of prayers for emotional strength. Samuel was not a happy camper when the Israelites asked for a king (1 Samuel 8:4-9). He took it somewhat personally and was suffering from the disease of rejection. In his distraught state, he turned to God in prayer. The Lord made it clear to him that they were not rejecting Samuel, but God Himself in asking for a king. Nevertheless, He had Samuel obey their request, but solemnly warn them about the consequences of their choice.

David also prayed for relief of emotional distress in Psalm 4 and received an answer from God. He declared that God had put more joy in his heart than when the grain and wine were in abundance. God also provided him with the peace to lie down and sleep.

Prayer for Healing

In addition to prayer for physical and emotional strength, we also have examples in the Bible of prayer for outright healing of disease. Abimelech's wife suffered from infertility because Abimelech had taken Abraham's wife Sarah as his own. When Abraham prayed for Abimelech, his wife and female slaves were healed so they could bear children (Genesis 20:17-18). Similarly, Isaac prayed for Rebecca when she was barren, and she was made able to conceive (Genesis 25:21). In fact, she had twins.

When King Jereboam tried to seize a man of God who was prophesying about the altar, his hand dried up so that he could not draw it back to himself. Upon realizing this, the king begged the man to pray to God for restoration of his hand. The king's hand was restored and became as it was before (1 Kings 13:4-6).

The Apostle Paul lost his vision on the road to Damascus during his conversion experience. He was told to go to Damascus and find a man named Ananias, who lived on Straight Street. Ananias had been forewarned that Paul was coming, but he was somewhat skeptical about greeting him because of Paul's reputation for persecuting Christians. Nevertheless, Ananias acted in faith and laid his hands on Paul and prayed for the return of his vision. Immediately, something like scales fell from Paul's eyes and his sight was restored (Acts 9:1-19).

Later, on the island of Malta, Paul met a chief man named Publius, whose father suffered from fever and dysentery. Paul visited him, prayed for him while laying his hands on him, and healed him. He also cured other people on the island of their diseases as well (Acts 28:7-10).

Sometimes we may feel like prayer is futile when a sick person has a very poor prognosis, such as terminal cancer. God is powerful, however, and there is no limit to His power to heal, if that is His will. Hezekiah had a terminal illness and was at the point of death. Because of his prayer and faith, however, he was granted an additional fifteen years to live (2 Kings 20:1-6; Isaiah 38:1-6). The power of God to heal fatal illnesses is described in Psalms 88 and 102 as well. And if that's not enough, Elisha prayed for healing of the Shummanite's son even after he was dead, and the child came back to life (1 Kings 4:32-37).

We should never disrespect God's power to heal, regardless of the severity of the illness. But by the same token, we should respect God's will, even if it is difficult for us to accept and understand. This is where faith comes in.

7

Prayer For Wisdom And Insight

The Bible also instructs us to pray for wisdom and insight. This would include both basic knowledge and understanding, as well as how to interpret or apply such knowledge in our daily living. Knowledge is simply being able to ascertain what is right and true, but wisdom is right knowledge used in association with right judgment. It is certainly possible to have knowledge without wisdom. Much of what we find in Scripture deals with its application. Sometimes we simply need some direction or insight from God about a decision or course of action, and it is very biblical to approach Him about this in prayer.

Often in the Bible we see people asking God for a sign with regard to a particular decision about what to do. Abraham's servant prayed for a sign as to whom he should marry and Rebekah was identified (Genesis 24:12-14). Elijah prayed for the very wet altar to be consumed with fire so people would recognize the power of God (1 Kings 18:36-38). And then there is Gideon's famous fleece test in Judges 6:36-40. This test was done in duplicate with altnating conditions to show Gideon that he would prevail with God's help.

But special signs are not required to gain basic knowledge and understanding from God. Manoah prayed for the return of an angel that had announced the impending birth of Samson to his wife

(Judges 13:8-14). David simply prayed that God would make him know the way he should go (Psalm 143:8). Saul prayed to ask God if he should pursue the Philistines (1 Sam 14:37-42). Jeremiah recognized his limitations for direction and asked God for correction (Jeremiah 10:23-25). The apostles prayed for God to show them who should take Judas' place, which He did as they cast lots (Acts 1:23-26).

More than just knowledge, what we often need from God is insight to appreciate the situations we are in and to apply the knowledge we already have. Elisha prayed for his servant to be able to see the spiritual forces that were present to assist them in their battle (2 Kings 6:15-17). This type of insight and understanding can come only from God. Jeremiah recognized this as he declared "great in counsel and mighty in deeds" (Jeremiah 32:18-19). Fortunately, if we lack wisdom, we can ask God for it; and, if we ask in faith, we will receive it (James 1:5-8).

The real question is *do we* ask for wisdom and insight as we live our daily lives before God? Do we see the same spiritual context in the events that occur in our lives as Elisha did, or are we blind to them as his servant was? Once we begin to view our lives in this spiritual context, we will be much more likely to recognize His great purposes and mighty deeds.

8

Prayer For Deliverance And Protection

There are numerous references in the Bible to prayer for deliverance and/or protection. People have prayed for deliverance from physical harm, forces of nature, sin, poor counsel, and humiliation. They have prayed for protection from both physical forces as well as the enemies of God. The Psalms are rich with prayers for deliverance and protection as we see in Psalms 35, 38-39, 40-44, 54, 56-57, 59-60, 64, 69-71, 77, 79, 81, 86, 88, 89:46-52, 90:13-17, 91, 102, 107, and 109.

Deliverance from Physical Harm

More passages deal with prayer for deliverance from physical harm than any other source of threat or danger. The most common source of physical harm in the Bible is from enemies, either physical or spiritual. Sometimes the enemy may be within the family, as was the case when Jacob prayed for deliverance from his brother, Esau (Genesis 32:11). He was conflicted because he knew God had promised to multiply his descendants, but he thought that Esau was going to kill him. His prayer was answered as Esau ran to meet him, embraced him, and kissed him.

Most commonly, however, prayers for deliverance from enemies have been offered up against foreigners or evil people. Elijah prayed to lose his life when confronted with Jezebel's threat to kill him

(1 Kings 19:4). He evidently preferred God taking it, to losing it to his enemy. Both Hezekiah and Isaiah prayed for deliverance from Sennacherib and the Assyrian army (2 Kings 19:3-7, 14-20; 2 Chronicles 32:20-22; Isaiah 37:14-22).

Sometimes we need deliverance more from spiritual enemies than from physical conquerors. David prayed for deliverance from his enemies who were "workers of evil" (Psalm 6; 55; 69:13-29; 143). He prayed for deliverance from wicked men whose portion was in this life (Psalm 17). He also prayed for deliverance from ruthless men who sought his life after every trouble (Psalm 54). The same prayer is offered by the apostle Paul in 2 Thessalonians 3:2. Paul also prayed for deliverance from unbelievers in Judea (Rom 15:30-33) and from deadly peril (2 Corinthians 1:10-11).

Other sources of physical harm include illness and imprisonment. As we have already noted, Hezekiah prayed for deliverance from his fatal illness and was given fifteen additional years to live (2 Kings 20:1-6). The sons of Korah prayed for deliverance from physical illness that had been present since their youth (Psalm 88, 102). Also, David prayed for deliverance from physical suffering as well as from wicked persecution (Psalm 109). The early church prayed for Peter's deliverance from prison (Acts 12:1-17). Both Paul and Silas prayed for deliverance from prison while they were held captive in both Philippi and Rome (Acts 16:16-28; Phil 1:18-19).

Deliverance from Forces of Nature

There are numerous examples in the Bible of prayers for deliverance from forces of nature. Many of these occur during the deliverance of the children of Israel from slavery in Egypt as Moses prayed for Pharaoh's deliverance from flies (Exodus 8:30), thunder and hail (Exodus 9:27-35), and locusts (Exodus 10:16-20). Moses also prayed for fiery serpents to be taken away from the children of Israel (Numbers 21:6-9). God answered by having him make a bronze serpent on a pole that they could look at and escape from harm.

We see prayers for deliverance from forces of nature in the New Testament as well. The sailors on Paul's ship enroute to Rome prayed for deliverance from the storm, the night, and shipwreck (Acts 27:27-35). In answer to their prayer, God delivered them safely to the island of Malta.

Deliverance from Sin

While forces of nature and physical harm can do substantial damage to our bodies and threaten our mortal lives, it is ultimately sin that causes us the most danger. Jesus warned, "And do not fear those who kill the body, but cannot kill the soul. Rather fear Him who can destroy both soul and body in hell" (Matthew 10:28). Sin separates us from God and destroys our relationship with Him. Since all have sinned and fall short of the glory of God, we find numerous references to prayer for deliverance from sin in the Bible.

When Aaron allowed the Israelites to make the golden calf and practice idolatry, the Lord was so angry with him and the people that He was ready to destroy all of them (Deuteronomy 9:13-29). Moses lay prostrate before the Lord, fasting for forty days and forty nights and prayed on behalf of Aaron and the Israelites. Because of Moses' prayer for deliverance on their behalf, the Lord relented and allowed them to continue to Canaan. Years later, the Israelites pleaded with Samuel to pray for God not to destroy them for having asked for a king (1 Samuel 12:19-25).

David also prayed for deliverance from the foolishness of his sin in taking a census, after being instructed against it (2 Samuel 24:10). This had cost the lives of 70,000 Israelites. On a more personal level, David prayed for deliverance from his individual sin with Bathsheba in Psalms 39 and 51. Also, while dedicating the temple, David's son Solomon prayed for deliverance from several consequences of sin (2 Chronicles 6:14-22; Daniel 9:3-23; 1 Kings 8:22-5). And in the New Testament, Paul prayed for the Corinthian Christians' deliverance from wrongdoing (2 Corinthians 13:7).

Deliverance from Poor Counsel and Humiliation

We may often have people seeking to give us advice who, while well-intentioned, may not be actually providing the best direction for our lives. Conversely, Satan may choose to use certain people in our lives to guide us away from God and toward his desires for us. Such was the case for David when Ahithophel conspired against him to promote Absalom, his son, as king. David prayed that Ahithophel's counsel would be turned into foolishness (2 Samuel 15:30-31). God used Husai the Archite to provide counsel against Ahithophel, ultimately leading to both his and Absalom's death.

Sometimes the outcome of our actions may not be quite what we want or cause us embarrassment or humiliation. This was the predicament that Jonah found himself in (Jonah 4:1-3). When directed by God to preach repentance to the people in Nineveh, he initially set out in the opposite direction in open defiance against God. Three days in the belly of a great fish changed his attitude somewhat, so he ultimately did go and do as he had been instructed. Unfortunately, (or so he perceived it), he was successful. The people of Nineveh repented, and God relented from the calamity He was about to send upon them. This actually made Jonah angry, and he was so upset about it, he prayed for God to take his life rather than face the outcome of what he had accomplished. Fortunately for him, this was a prayer that God chose not to answer, but it does illustrate how we can take situations like this to our Father for consideration.

Prayer for Protection

In addition to prayers for deliverance, we also find people in the Bible being proactive and praying for protection in several situations. When surrounded by hostile forces, Elisha prayed for the Syrians to be struck with blindness (2 Kings 6:18). Nehemiah prayed for both deliverance from the taunts of Sanballet and Tobiah as well as for protection from them (Nehemiah 4:4-9). David also prayed for protection for all who take refuge in God (Psalm 16). These examples should encourage us to be proactive in prayer and pray for protection as well as for deliverance.

9

Prayer For Justice And Judgment

In addition to prayer for physical and emotional strength, wisdom and insight, and deliverance and protection, the Bible also presents us with several examples of prayer for justice and judgment. We have already alluded to Samson's prayer, which was in essence a prayer for revenge (Judges 16:28-30). God answered Samson's prayer to bring judgment upon his captors.

Prayers of Nehemiah for Justice

Nehemiah also prayed prayers of vengeance for justice. When opposed by Sanballet and Tobiah in rebuilding the wall, Nehemiah prayed that their guilt would not be covered and their sins would not be blotted out (Nehemiah 4:4-5). He also prayed for increased strength to deal with their taunts and fear (Nehemiah 6:9-14). Later he prayed for the sons of Jehoida to be remembered and avenged for desecrating the priesthood (Nehemiah 13:28-29).

Prayers of David and Solomon for Justice

Both David and Solomon also prayed for vengeance and justice in various situations. David prayed for vindication from malicious or violent witnesses when they repaid him evil for good (Psalm 35:11-26). When they were sick, he had prayed and fasted for them, but they rejoiced at his stumbling. So David prayed for them to be put to shame, dishonor, and disappointment. David also had the confidence to ask God to vindicate him for his blameless life (Psalm 27:1-4). Solomon prayed that if someone wronged another person and was required to take an oath of innocence, that God would hear and punish the wrongdoer (2 Chronicles 6:22-23; 1 Kings 8:31-32).

What About Us?

What about us? Is it appropriate to ask God to bring judgment or vengeance upon those who would trouble us or do us harm? I believe these examples suggest it is. Our God is a just God. Asking for justice is in accordance with His divine nature. However, we must be sure that our cause is truly just.

We are told by Jesus not to judge others. Generally speaking, we tend not to be very good judges. Unlike God, we do not always know peoples' hearts and motives and therefore are likely to make bad judgments. That's why it may sometime be best to be content with "Vengeance is mine, I will repay," says the Lord (Romans 12:19).

Praying for vengeance or justice may also seem to contradict Jesus' admonition to love our enemies. Did He not say that we should pray for those who persecute us (Matthew 5:44)? These two prayers are not necessarily in conflict. If we are truly experiencing injustice, the source of that injustice must not be in alignment with God's will, since God is just. Before his capture and death, I prayed daily for Osama bin Laden to overcome the deception that Satan had deceived him with and to come to know Jesus and be saved. But at the same time, I also prayed for justice for all who have suffered from terrorists and that those individuals responsible would be held accountable for their crimes. With respect to Mr. bin Laden, it was the latter prayer that was answered.

Political Justice

Paul instructed Timothy to pray for kings and all who are in authority (1 Timothy 2:1,2). But what should we be praying about for them? In Psalm 72, David prays for Solomon as king to judge the people with righteousness and the poor with justice. Our political leaders have great power to bring relief and help to those who are needy or to oppress them and enrich themselves. David recognized this and made it a focus of his prayer for King Solomon. He even asked that prayer be made for him continually and blessings be invoked for him all day. We should be so diligent in praying for our elected leaders and the success of their administrations in providing social justice.

10

Prayer For Blessings

We find numerous prayers in the Bible asking for the blessings of God. Sometimes this is requested in a general sense. But sometimes specific blessings are requested as well. There are prayers for the blessing of fulfillment, success, living in the presence of God, and peace. Let's examine each of these individually.

General Blessings of God

Both David and Nehemiah offered prayers to God requesting His blessings in very general ways. David prayed for blessings on his house that it might continue forever (2 Samuel 7:18-29). In Psalm 61, David prayed for his years to be prolonged with steadfast love and faithfulness. Nehemiah also prayed for blessings for himself because of his service before God (Nehemiah 13:14,22). We, too, should be seeking God and petitioning His blessings upon us.

Blessings of Fulfillment

As we saw in Samuel, David prayed for general blessings so that his house might continue forever. But he also prayed on other occasions more specifically for the fulfillment of his dynasty. In 1 Chronicles 17:23-25, David calls upon God to honor the promise He has made to establish his house forever. Of course, David probably had his physical dynasty in mind when he asked this of God. But God's answer came in terms of a spiritual dynasty through Jesus Christ, a direct descendant of David. This same request was later made by Solomon as he asked God to remember His promise to David (1 Kings 8:22-26; 2 Chronicles 6:12-17). We, too, have many great and precious promises from God. Our prayer should reflect this as we also pray for fulfillment of those promises.

Blessings of Success

We also should pray for God to bless us with success in whatever we aspire to do. Nehemiah provides a great example of that. When burdened with the plight of Jerusalem after the Babylonian captivity, Nehemiah prayed for success and mercy in going before King Artaxerxes to ask to return to rebuild the wall (Nehemiah 1:4-11; 2:4-6). This was not without some risk. Nehemiah was the cupbearer to the king. He was a captive with a prescribed task. There was no guarantee that Artaxerxes would be willing to relinquish his service for this task. But God answered Nehemiah's prayer and the wall in Jerusalem was rebuilt. Whatever we do should be done to the glory of God and we should always aspire to success and ask God's blessings upon our efforts.

The prayer of Jabez in 1 Chronicles 4:10 has been emphasized much in recent years through Bruce Wilkinson's book on this passage. This rather obscure man of God directly seeks God's blessings on his life as he cries out to God, "Oh, that you would bless me and enlarge my border, and that your hand might be with me, and that you would keep me from harm so that it might not bring me pain." And God granted his request. Do we have the faith to believe that God will do the same for us if we seek His blessings so directly with the same urgency?

Blessing of Living in the Presence of God

In Psalm 84, the sons of Korah recognized that those who lived with God, with Him as their strength and trust, were truly blessed. They go from strength to strength. The Lord bestows favor and honor upon them. Nothing good is withheld from them. Is this not what we want? Then this is the blessing that we should seek in prayer, as David did in Psalm 106:4. We should faint to be in His presence. We should sing for joy and praise Him for His blessings (Psalm 67). Truly it is better to be the doorkeeper in the house of God than to dwell in the tents of wickedness (Psalm 84:10).

The Blessing of Peace

A final blessing we should seek from God is the blessing of peace. This blessing has many perspectives. In Psalm 122, David prayed for the peace of Jerusalem. This was requested from a perspective of safety and security for the people of God. Most of us today enjoy relative peace from this perspective, although some Christians in other parts of the world do not. We should certainly pray for them.

But for ourselves, it is more internal peace that we might desire—peace of mind, peace of our emotions, and peace of Spirit. These, too, are blessings that we can seek from God. Just as He can provide safety and security to His people in Jerusalem, He can also provide peace from the spiritual war we engage in each day, as we strive to follow God's will amid Satan's efforts to distract and dissuade us.

11

Prayer For Confession And Repentance

Given the human propensity for sin, it's not surprising that many prayers in the Bible involve expressions of confession and repentance toward God. These prayers should be frequent, as they reflect a proper understanding of our inadequacy and failure before a holy God. A broken and contrite heart He will not despise. (Psalm 51:17).

Prayers of Confession

We have three excellent examples of prayers of this type from David, Ezra, and Nehemiah. Psalm 51 recounts David's confession of his adulterous and murderous sin with Bathsheba. He laments, "For I know my transgressions, and my sin is ever before me. Against you, you only, have I sinned and done what is evil in your sight, so that you may be justified in your words and blameless in your judgment. Behold, I was brought forth in iniquity, and in sin did my mother conceive me" (Psalm 51:3-5).

In 458 BC, Ezra led a second wave of Israelites from Babylon back to Jerusalem to rebuild the temple after Zerubbabel had earlier led a first wave in 538 BC. They completed the work, celebrated Passover, and sacrificed offerings to God. But the men also began to intermarry with the local women there, including the priests and Levites. This prompted Ezra to pray, "O my God, I am ashamed and blush to lift my face to you, my God, for our iniquities have risen higher than our heads and our guilt has mounted up the heavens" (Ezra 9:6). His prayer caused a great number of men, women, and children to assemble and weep bitterly. Even the sons of the priests pledged themselves to put away their foreign wives.

One might think such ardent prayer and response would keep the people from lapsing back into disobedience in the future. Think again. The ninth and tenth chapters of Nehemiah record the confession and prayer of a third wave of the children of Israel after returning to Jerusalem from Babylonian captivity. They demonstrated their penitence by fasting and wearing sackcloth or putting dirt on their heads, common signs of regret and remorse in those times. They spent a quarter of a day reading the Book of the Law and another quarter of the day in confession and worship. Their prayer, beginning in verse 6, chronicled all that God had done for them since creation and the establishment of the covenant through Abraham. They also confessed their failings in obedience and praised God's consistent faithfulness throughout their varied circumstances. Ultimately this led to the signing of a formal covenant to recommit themselves to following God's law.

Have you ever spent a quarter of a day in prayer? Or have you ever verbalized all the Lord has done for you since birth and confessed all the times that you have been disobedient? That would probably require a quarter of a day, if not more! But these people were serious about their penitence. And it was reflected in their prayer life. Does your prayer life reflect an understanding of your inadequacy and failure before God?

Prayers of Repentance

In addition to these examples of prayers of confession, we also have a few examples of prayers for repentance in the Bible. Confession and repentance are integrally linked. Repentance is a change of heart and action based upon confession of sin. It's not just saying, "I'm sorry." It literally means turning and going 180 degrees in the opposite direction. For most of us, this is not easy. It's only with the help of God that we can truly "put to death the deeds of the body," as Paul said (Romans 8:13).

David expresses repentance in Psalm 51 as well. Upon receiving God's cleansing and restoration, he states, "Then I will teach transgressors your ways, and sinners will return to you (Psalm 51:13). He also pledges to sing aloud of God's righteousness and declare His praise.

Manasseh also provides a great example of praying for repentance (2 Chronicles 33:1-20). Manasseh was not a particularly great king for Judah. His father, Hezekiah, had brought great religious reform to Judah by cleaning up the land and removing all the altars of idolatry to other gods. But Manasseh did what was evil in the sight of the Lord and rebuilt the high places that his father had torn down and erected altars to other false gods, such as Baal and Asherah. He also dealt in sorcery and mediums and even offered his two sons as a burnt sacrifice to false gods. This provoked the Lord to anger.

The Lord spoke to Manasseh and his people about this, but they paid no attention. So God promptly sent commanders from the king of Assyria who captured Manasseh with hooks and took him back to Babylon in bronze chains. Guess that got his attention!

At this point Manasseh entreated the favor of the Lord his God and humbled himself greatly before Him. He prayed to Him and God was moved by his entreaty and returned him to his kingdom in Jerusalem.

After this prayer and its subsequent answer, Manasseh appears to be a changed man. He rebuilds the outer wall of Jerusalem and puts commanders in the fortified cities of Judah. He takes away all the foreign gods and idols and altars that he had built. He restores the altar of the Lord and reinstitutes proper worship and offers sacrifices of peace and thanksgiving and commands all of Judah to do the same.

I think Manasseh gives us a lot of hope. If one can be so far away from God as to sacrifice his own children in fire and still be able to pray for repentance and mercy with a positive response from God, surely God will answer us when we mess up. As they say, "All's well that ends well," and in the case of Manasseh, his repentance appears to be genuine and the story has a happy ending as he dies and goes to rest with his fathers.

Prayer For Mercy And Forgiveness

Another great need common to man for which we can pray is the need for mercy and forgiveness. We have a need for mercy and forgiveness ourselves because of our sin, and we have a need to be able to show mercy and forgive those who sin against us. Fortunately, the Bible offers us examples of prayer for each of these.

Prayer for Personal Mercy and Forgiveness

The Psalms are replete with prayers to God for mercy. Psalm 28 begins, "Hear the voice of my pleas for mercy when I cry to you for help, when I lift up my hands toward your sanctuary" (Psalms 28:2). Just four verses later the Psalmist declares, "Blessed be the LORD, for he has heard the voice of my pleas for mercy" (Psalms 28:6). Similar language can be found in Psalms 30:8-10; 51; 55; 57; 80; 85; and 86:3.

Nehemiah asked God to remember his faithfulness and show mercy to him (Nehemiah 13:14-29). He also asked God to remember the unfaithfulness of the house of Jehoida and seems to not want mercy shown to them. David prayed for God to be gracious to him when he was languishing physically (Psalm 6). One of the greatest characteristics of our God is His merciful nature, and we should not be timid about seeking His mercy in our time of need.

When Solomon prayed at the dedication of the temple he had built for God, he prayed several times for the forgiveness of the people for individual sins (2 Chronicles 6:24-40). In each situation, they had experienced negative consequences because of their sin: defeat from enemies, lack of rain, famine, and captivity. In each case Solomon specifies that they must turn again to God, acknowledge His name, and pray and plead with Him in order to receive forgiveness. But Solomon appears confident that God will accept sincere penitence and provide forgiveness. We must be willing to do the same, if we hope to be forgiven when we find ourselves in sin.

Similarly, Isaiah prays for his personal sin before God as well as for the people of Judah (Isaiah 64:5-9). This sin appears to have been going on for some time. He describes the people as "polluted garments" or a shriveled leaf about to be blown away by the wind. No one calls upon the name of God. And because of this, God has hidden His face from them. But Isaiah beseeches the Lord "be not so terribly angry" and "remember not iniquity forever."

These passages illustrate the need for repentance and its relationship to prayer. But what if people have not repented of their sin? What if they still persist in it or have not fully changed their ways? Is there any point in praying for mercy and forgiveness in this situation?

Good King Hezekiah provides some insight in this regard. In 2 Chronicles 30, Hezekiah sent couriers all over Israel and Judah, calling the people to come celebrate Passover in Jerusalem. Many people came, but a great number in the assembly had not consecrated themselves appropriately according to their law. The Levites had to slaughter a Passover lamb for everyone who was unclean. Hezekiah prayed, "May the good Lord pardon everyone who sets his heart to seek God, the Lord, the God of his fathers, even though not according to the sanctuary's rules of cleanness." And the Lord heard Hezekiah and healed the people.

Prayer for Those Who Sin Against Us

Perhaps what's more difficult than praying for forgiveness for our own sin, is praying for people who sin against us. But the Bible clearly directs us to do this. Jesus tells us in the Sermon on the Mount that we should love our enemies and pray for those who persecute us (Matthew 5:44). In the Lord's prayer, Jesus teaches the disciples to pray, "…forgive us our debts, as we also have forgiven our debtors" (Matthew 6:12). This is consistent with the principle that we are forgiven ourselves to the extent that we are willing to forgive others. But Jesus does more than just teach these things. In perhaps the greatest demonstration of selfless prayer ever, while dying on the cross, Jesus himself prays, "Father, forgive them, for they know not what they do" (Luke 23:34). Oh for the mercy and compassion for us to pray as He did.

13

Prayer For Praise
And Thanksgiving

A final type of prayer we find several examples of in the Bible is prayer for praise and thanksgiving. Surely all of us can pray this prayer if we reflect but a moment on all the blessings that God has given us. The problem with this prayer might be in knowing when to stop. (Psalm 40:5). God is gracious and has been too good to all of us.

Prayer of Praise

There are innumerable reasons why we should praise God in prayer. I praise His divine nature in that He is constant and unchanging. I praise the way He has revealed Himself to us through His Word. And, of course, I praise Him for his love in sending His only begotten Son to show us what He is like, to teach us how to live, and to atone for our sin. I praise Jesus for His obedience, submission, and humility to give up the glory of heaven and endure life in a human body, experiencing pain, ridicule, torture, rejection, and ultimately separation from God for my sin. I praise His Holy Spirit for raising Jesus from the dead and for living in me as a down payment for the hope I have of resurrection as well. I also praise the Holy Spirit for preserving the record of all of this for me through two thousand years of human history, so I might know, believe, and be saved through my faith in Him. Solomon recognized that there was no god like God and that heaven and all the heavens could not contain Him (2 Chronicles 6:14).

If we really concentrate on how God has blessed us, we could probably all pray 24/7, just praising Him for this. Unfortunately, I sense that most of us don't praise Him nearly as much as we should, or as much as He deserves. That's kind of hard to explain. I suppose in our human condition, we just take things for granted and often fail to realize the Source of all we have. Or maybe we are just too distracted by worldly matters to focus on the reality of our salvation. God, forgive us for our ingratitude.

Hannah exulted in the LORD and rejoiced over her salvation (1 Samuel 2:1-10). And she enumerated several reasons why. She recognized His holiness. She revered Him as the source of truth and right judgment. She saw how God cared for the poor and humble. Yet she recognized His power to kill or give life or to bring low or exalt. And, ultimately, she perceived God's faithfulness to those who were His, but vengeance against those who reject Him.

Our praise to God in prayer should be constant. Too often, however, when all is well, we tend to accept God's blessings but neglect to praise Him for them. And when things are not so well, we seek Him out for deliverance and relief, but do we remember to praise Him then as well? Consider Habakkuk's example. In spite of famine and loss of livestock, Habakkuk could rejoice in the LORD and take joy in the God of his salvation (Habakkuk 3:17-19).

Prayer of Thanksgiving

Just as we have many things for which to praise God, we also have many things for which to thank Him. These prayers are so closely related, they are often referred to as a single "prayer of praise and thanksgiving" in the Bible. Paul used this terminology quite frequently in his writing.

And just as there is no limit to what we should praise God for, there is also no limit for that for which we should be thankful. But we do have several specific examples of this in the Bible.

David was thankful for God revealing his future to him and showing him that his kingdom would be established forever (1 Chronicles 17:16-27). He was also thankful when God turned his wailing into dancing (Psalms 30:11-12). Jonah sacrificed with the voice of thanksgiving and kept his vow and rejoiced in his salvation (Jonah 2:1-9). When about to be shipwrecked, Paul took bread, gave thanks, and broke it with the other sailors for food (Acts 27:27-35). But Paul knew God would ultimately provide for them and that not a hair on the head of any of them would perish. So there are always things for which we can be thankful, even in the direst situations. Thankfulness is ultimately an attitude of our heart that reflects our faith and trust in God and willingness to give Him the glory for all that we have and do.

No one has said it better than the Psalmists and the Psalms are replete with praise and thanksgiving. For example, in Psalm 57:5-11, David writes, "Be exalted, O God, above the heavens! Let your glory be over all the earth! They set a net for my steps—my soul was bowed down. They dug a pit in my way—but they have fallen

into it themselves. Selah My heart is steadfast, O God, my heart is steadfast! I will sing and make melody. Awake, my glory! Awake, harp and lyre! I will awake the dawn. I will give thanks to you, O Lord, among the peoples; I will sing praises to you among the nations. For your steadfast love is great to the heavens; your faithfulness to the clouds. Be exalted, O God, above the heavens! Let your glory be over all the earth!" Additional prayers of praise and thanksgiving can be found in Psalms 59:16-17; 66; 75; 76; 86:12-13; 89:5-18; 92; 97:9-12; 100; and 103-108.

Afterword

So what now? You've seen that the Bible has a lot to say about prayer. You've learned about its meaning, some characteristics of prayer, its nature, and even some prerequisites that are necessary for prayer. You've learned many things about how to pray and the many types of prayers that you can offer up to God.

But so what? Will this study transform your life as it has mine, or will this simply be just another book to set up on the shelf with all the others? The decision is yours.

Let me make a few suggestions in that regard. If you truly want a closer personal relationship with God in prayer, then stop right now and ask Him for that. That's exactly how this book began. Then I would encourage you to set aside a specific time and place for daily prayer with God. It's fine to continue to have short prayers throughout the day while you work or drive or exercise, but you really need to have some time dedicated to God alone and for Him only. It doesn't have to be an extraordinarily long time, but it does have to be a quiet place where you can focus on Him without interruption. As you reap the benefit of this relationship, you will find you will want to spend more and more time with Him in prayer; and that may require some adjustment to your daily schedule. As I mentioned in the book, a good prayer life, like everything else in life, requires effort and discipline, but the rewards are well worth it.

I would also recommend you start a list of things to pray about. I have my list broken down into sections such as family and friends, people who are shut-ins, spiritual needs, suffering and bereavement, physical needs, and miscellaneous things. Oh yes, and don't forget to have a section for praise and thanksgiving. That way, as your prayers are answered, you can cross them off and put them in that section. Keep your prayer list with you as much as possible. Listen for things to pray for when you listen to the radio or watch TV or read the newspaper. You'll be amazed how fast that list will grow and you will be actively engaged in the lives of other people, lifting them up before God and watching Him work in their lives!

As you begin to pray, try to include as many of the different forms of prayer as you can. At some times in your life, prayer for deliverance or physical and emotional strength may be more important than at other times. But you should always have prayer for praise and thanksgiving, wisdom and understanding, and blessings. The main thing is keeping an active conversation going with God and opening yourself up to Him by humbling yourself and being honest with Him about your circumstances. I guarantee you will not be disappointed! In fact, if you're like me, you will regret that you never took your prayer life seriously earlier in your life and missed out on many years of a fantastic experience with God. It is my prayer for you that you will come to know and love the precious encounter of man and God that occurs in the secret place of thunder.

Study Guide

1

The Meaning Of Prayer

REFLECTION

1. When have you struggled with prayer? What did that look like? How did it feel?

2. What words would you use to describe prayer to someone who didn't know what it was?

3. Does the quality of your prayer life fit the definition of prayer that we see in the original Hebrew and Greek words?

SCRIPTURES TO CONSIDER

Genesis 20:3-7 _____

_____

Matthew 26:52-53 _____

_____

Matthew 9:38 _____

_____

Matthew 21:22 _____

_____

Hebrews 4:16 _____

_____

THINGS TO THINK AND TALK ABOUT

1. Why was it necessary for Abraham to pray for Abimelek when he returned Sarah to him?

2. Who can you *parakaleo* when you need help?

3. What things have you begged God for? Are they more likely to be spiritual things or physical things?

4. Did Jesus *really* mean we will receive whatever we ask for in prayer, if we ask in faith?

5. Do you feel comfortable approaching God in prayer with confidence? Why or why not?

2

The Nature Of Prayer

RELFECTION

1. How would you characterize your own prayer life?
2. Do the characteristics of prayer found in the Bible apply to your prayer life?
3. Do you view prayer as simply a "means to an end?"
4. How have you felt and responded when your prayers were not answered right away?

SCRIPTURES TO CONSIDER

Luke 22:41-44 _____

_____

Daniel 6:10 _____

_____

Jeremiah 29:13 _____

_____

1 Samuel 12:23 _____

_____

Mark 14:38 _____

_____

Luke 18:1-8 _____

_____

Lamentations 3:42-44 _____

_____

THINGS TO THINK AND TALK ABOUT

1. When in your life have you prayed with great emotion?
2. On a scale of 1 to 10, how much effort do you put into your prayer life?
3. Have you viewed failure to pray for someone as sin?
4. What are some spiritual needs that you pray for?
5. Describe a time when you felt God did not hear or answer your prayer.
6. How persistent have you been in prayer?
7. Have you ever considered sin as an explanation for unanswered prayer in your life?

3

The Focus Of Prayer

REFLECTION

1. How much of your prayer time is spent praying for other people, especially unbelievers? Is it more about physical needs or spiritual needs?

2. Do you pray regularly for believers? If so, what spiritual needs of other believers do you pray for? 3. And how about yourself? Do you pray more for your own physical needs or spiritual needs?

SCRIPTURES TO CONSIDER

1 Timothy 2:1-2 _____

_____

James 5:17-18 _____

_____

Romans 10:1 _____

_____

Matthew 5:43-44 _____

_____

James 5:14-16 _____

_____

Colossians 1:9-12 _____

_____

Romans 15:30-32_____

_____

Luke 22:40_____

_____

THINGS TO THINK AND TALK ABOUT

1. What are some specific things you have prayed about for unbelievers, both physical and spiritual?

2. What do you want other Christians to pray about for you?

3. Do you pray more about physical needs or spiritual needs for other Christians?

4. What do you pray mostly about for yourself?

5. How do current events in the media inform your prayer life?

4

Prerequisites For Prayer

REFLECTION

1. Have you ever considered what is necessary for an effective prayer life? Or have you just taken it for granted that if you wanted to pray, God must be willing to hear you?

2. Do you agree that the five qualities discussed in this chapter are imperative to effective prayer?

3. How can you better incorporate these qualities into your life?

SCRIPTURES TO CONSIDER

2 Chronicles 7:12-14 _____

_____

Luke 20:46-47 _____

_____

Mark 11:25 _____

_____

1 Chronicles 17:25 _____

_____

THINGS TO THINK AND TALK ABOUT

1. What are some practical ways in which you can show humility before God?

2. Why is repentance necessary for effective prayer?

3. What is the relationship between repentance and obedience with regard to their impact on our prayer life?

4. Why is it so hard to forgive those who have hurt us, yet so necessary for effective prayer?

5. Describe how you have been courageous in prayer.

5

How To Pray

REFLECTION

1. How much thought have you given to how you pray?
2. Have you considered the amount of time you spend in prayer or the frequency of it?
3. Have you thought about where you pray or your posture during prayer? Are you surprised that the Bible addresses these issues in a very specific way?

SCRIPTURES TO CONSIDER

Acts 16:13 _____

_____

Acts 3:1 _____

_____

Matthew 6:6 _____

_____

Acts 10:9 _____

_____

Psalm 55:17 _____

_____

1 Corinthians 7:5 _____

_____

Deuteronomy 9:25 _____

_____

2 Kings 20:2 _____

_____

Luke 22:44_____

_____

Luke 6:12_____

_____

Matthew 7:7 _____

_____

THINGS TO THINK AND TALK ABOUT

1. Do have a special place that you go to pray?
   If not, where could you go?

2. Do you have a dedicated period of time to pray to God each
   day and also pray shorter prayers throughout the day?
   Could this be a realistic way of life for you?

3. What is your favorite position for prayer? Why?

4. Do you maintain an active prayer list? If not, could this be a simple
   but effective way to focus your prayers?

5. Do you become emotional when in prayer?

6. What is the longest period of time you have prayed?

7. Why does God tell us to pray if He already knows everything
   anyway?

8. How is the Lord's Prayer a good model for us to follow?

6

Prayer For Physical
And Emotional Strength

REFLECTION

1. When have you prayed for physical or emotional strength? Were there particular circumstances that led you to do this? Or is this part of your regular prayer life?

2. Often we neglect to go to God for healing except in times of extreme circumstances. Have you ever felt your prayer was futile such as when people have a terminal disease?

3. Do you really have the faith to believe that God can still heal even under those dire circumstances?

SCRIPTURES TO CONSIDER

Luke 22:42 _____

_____

Judges 16:29 _____

_____

Psalm 4:1 _____

_____

Gen 25:21 _____

_____

Acts 28:7-9 _____

_____

2 Kings 20:1-6 _____

_____

THINGS TO THINK AND TALK ABOUT

1. How does Jesus' prayer when He was suffering in Gethsemane inform our prayer life when we are suffering?

2. Is it appropriate to pray for revenge as Samson did?

3. In what ways can prayer help us deal with emotional distress?

4. How do you feel about praying for full and complete healing for someone who has a terminal diagnosis?

5. When should you stop praying for healing in times like this?

7

Prayer For Wisdom And Insight

REFLECTION

1. How often have you prayed for wisdom and insight in your life?

2. Have you typically viewed your life in a spiritual context with the events that happen as a part of God's greater plan? Or are you more likely to write off things to circumstances or luck?

3. In retrospect, have there been situations in your life when you wish you had prayed for wisdom and insight?

SCRIPTURES TO CONSIDER

Genesis 24:12-14 _____

_____

Psalm 143:8 _____

_____

2 Kings 6:15-17 _____

_____

James 1:5-8 _____

_____

THINGS TO THINK AND TALK ABOUT

1. Have you ever asked God for a sign about something?

2. Can we receive direction from God without some special sign? If so, how might this happen?

3. How would you describe the difference in wisdom and insight?

4. Which is more important in your life?

5. Describe how you have seen God's great purposes and mighty deeds at work in your life.

8

Prayer For Deliverance And Protection

REFLECTION

1. For what things in your life do you need deliverance and/or protection? Have you brought these to God's attention in prayer?

2. Are your needs more spiritual or physical, or both?

3. Do you believe that God can and will deliver you from these things?

4. What is your role in being delivered by God?

SCRIPTURES TO CONSIDER

Genesis 32:11 _____

_____

1 Kings 19:3-4 _____

_____

2 Corinthians 1:10-11 _____

_____

Philippians 1:18-19 _____

_____

2 Samuel 24:10_____

_____

2 Corinthians 13:7 _____

_____

Jonah 4:1-3 _____

_____

Psalm 16:1-2 _____

_____

THINGS TO THINK AND TALK ABOUT

1. What are some family issues that might require prayer for deliverance?

2. From what evil forces around you do you need deliverance?

3. How can physical suffering or forces of nature require prayer for deliverance?

4. Why is sin our greatest need for deliverance?

5. Have you ever needed deliverance from poor counsel or humiliation?

6. What is the difference between prayer for protection and prayer for deliverance?

9

Prayer For Justice And Judgment

REFLECTION

1. When have you suffered from injustice? Did you feel like praying about it?
2. Does it seem wrong to pray for retribution to others who may have treated you unfairly?
3. How confident are you in your ability to judge correctly in these situations?
4. Why do you think that Jesus taught us to "judge not?"

SCRIPTURES TO CONSIDER

Judges 16:28 _____

_____

Nehemiah 4:4-5 _____

_____

Psalm 35:26 _____

_____

2 Chron 6:22-23 _____

_____

Psalm 72:1-2_____

_____

THINGS TO THINK AND TALK ABOUT

1. Describe a time in your life you suffered injustice.
   How did you deal with it?

2. What would you pray if you were being unjustly opposed by
   another person? Another Christian?

3. Have you ever prayed for others only to have them treat you
   unjustly later? How would that make you feel?

4. Do you feel comfortable in asking God to punish wrongdoers?
   Why or why not?

5. Is this in conflict with Jesus' teaching that we should love our
   enemies and pray for those who persecute us?

6. What are ways in which our elected officials can judge with justice
   and righteousness?

10

Prayer For Blessings

REFLECTION

1. How has God blessed your life? Do you actively seek His continued blessing in your life or do you simply take His blessings for granted? Do you believe your life could be even more blessed if you sought His blessings more actively? What other kinds of blessings would you like to receive from God?

SCRIPTURES TO CONSIDER

2 Samuel 7:25-26 _____

_____

Nehemiah 13:14 _____

_____

1 Chronicles 17:23-24 _____

_____

Nehemiah 2:4-5 _____

_____

1 Chronicles 4:10 _____

_____

Psalm 84:8-10_____

_____

Psalm 122:6 _____

_____

THINKS TO THINK AND TALK ABOUT

1. For what general blessings from God do you pray?

2. What specific promises of God would you pray for fulfillment?

3. Do you feel comfortable asking God to grant you success in whatever you do? Why or why not?

4. Can you relate to the blessing of living in the presence of God as expressed in Psalm 84?

5. What is the blessing of peace that is needed in your life?

11

Prayer For Confession And Repentance

REFLECTION

1. How often do you confess sin before God in prayer? Is this easy or difficult for you?

2. How do you feel when you confess? How do you feel afterwards?

3. Does confession ever cause you to weep bitterly as Ezra did?

4. How much time do you spend in confession and repentance?

5. Do you find yourself confessing the same sin(s) over and over again? How do you think God feels about that?

SCRIPTURES TO CONSIDER

Psalm 51:3-4 _____

_____

Ezra 9:6 _____

_____

Nehemiah 9:3 _____

_____

Nehemiah 9:32-33 _____

_____

2 Chronicles 33:12-13 _____

_____

THINGS TO THINK AND TALK ABOUT

1. What does it mean to have a "broken and contrite heart"?

2. Which prayer of confession do you relate to the most, that of David, Ezra, or Nehemiah? Why?

3. What does the amount of time we spend in prayer tell us about our sincerity?

4. What does repentance mean?

5. Is it possible to truly "put to death the misdeeds of the body?"

6. What makes Manasseh's repentance so remarkable?

12

Prayer For Mercy And Forgiveness

REFLECTION

1. When in your life have you found yourself in need of mercy and forgiveness? What was that like?

2. Did you feel God was accessible to you at that time? 3. Did you cry out to Him as the Psalmists so often do? Or have you found yourself at the other end of the spectrum – needing to give mercy and forgiveness to someone who had offended or hurt you?

4. Was that any easier? And was God involved in that process as well?

SCRIPTURES TO CONSIDER

Psalms 28:6-7 _____

_____

Psalms 6:8-9 _____

_____

2 Chronicles 6:24-25 _____

_____

Isaiah 64:5-6,9 _____

_____

2 Chronicles 30:18-19 _____

_____

Matthew 6:12 _____

_____

Luke 23:34_____

_____

THINGS TO THINK AND TALK ABOUT

1. What are some things for which we might cry to God for mercy?

2. Can we barter faithfulness with God for mercy?
   (See Nehemiah 13:14-29).

3. What do Solomon and Isaiah teach us about God's tolerance and forgiveness of perpetual sin?

4. Why do you think God answered Hezekiah's prayer for the people who were ceremonially unclean?

5. Why is it imperative for us to show mercy and forgiveness to others?

13

Prayer For Praise And Thanksgiving

REFLECTION

1. How often do you offer prayers that are primarily praise and thanksgiving? Is this a constant feature of your prayer life? Why or why not?

2. What are some reasons why you should praise God?

3. For what things in your life are you thankful?

4. Why are praise and thanksgiving so complementary in prayer?

5. Does God need our praise or our thanks? Why do you think He might desire it?

SCRIPTURES TO CONSIDER

2 Chronicles 6:13-14 _____

_____

1 Samuel 2:1-2 _____

_____

Psalms 30:11-12 _____

_____

Acts 27:27-35 _____

_____

Psalms 107:1 _____

_____

THINGS TO THINK AND TALK ABOUT

1. Describe some ways in which you praise God in prayer.

2. What prompted Solomon and Hannah to praise Him?

3. Tell about a time you were able to praise God in spite of some difficulty or hardship like Habakkuk.

4. What are some things you are thankful for?

5. Do you regularly give thanks before eating? Why or why not?

6. Which of the Psalms of praise and thanksgiving is most meaningful to you and why?

CPSIA information can be obtained at www.ICGtesting.com
Printed in the USA
LVOW121033140613

338593LV00006B/8/P